A trip to Milan

The day of the trip has finally arrived. Departure at eight o'clock. The children from class 5B shout and push to get on the coach parked in front of the school. The last to get on is Mira. For a moment all the children turn round to see where she is going to sit. She has no choice as the only seat left is the one beside Archimedes.

Mira sits down and everyone starts laughing, shouting and making a racket again. Only Archimedes sits silently while his face gets as red as a beetroot. He is not happy about having to sit beside that strange girl.

She glances at him and then stares in front of her.

Mira has been in 5B only a couple of weeks, and since the first day everyone has noticed that she is different. Since she arrived in class something always happens; like when Master Luc's chalk stuck to the blackboard, or when the last exercise disappeared from everyone's maths book.

Mira is said to live alone with her grandmother in a big house outside the village but no-one has ever been able to find it. Archimedes prefers not to think about it too much so as not to ruin his day out. A visit to the Science Museum in Milan is a fantastic thing for him. For weeks he has been reading his books on inventions to prepare himself for it.

I have to tell you that Archimedes is the most studious boy in the class. His name is not really Archimedes but, as he is always making strange experiments or dreaming about becoming an inventor, instead of playing with his school friends, they all call him by this name.

Archimedes' father is a railwayman and so they live in the old abandoned station of the village. Archimedes is lucky because not only has he got a lot of space to put his constructions, but there is a small square behind the station where he can find everything he needs: wrecks of cars and motorbikes, old train carriages which have been abandoned for years, dismantled train engines and enormous piles of old machinery. Since his father taught him how to weld there is no stopping him. It's only a pity that he always has to do everything alone. His school friends prefer to play football and he is no good at football.

In the Science Museum

After about an hour on the motorway and another hour in the wild traffic of Milan, the coach pulls up in front of the Science Museum and the visit begins.

The machines of Leonardo da Vinci are exhibited in a large gallery. The models were made from the drawings that Leonardo had done in his notebooks where he wrote his thoughts and inventions. While the teacher is telling the children about Leonardo Mira sits down on one of the machines. This is forbidden and there are even signs saying: "Don't touch". Mira calls Archimedes but he tries to ignore her.

Attention please children: Leonardo da Vinci was born in Anchiano, a small village near Vinci in the heart of Tuscany in 1452. Gianni be silent! He lived in Vinci until he was 17 years old and then he moved to Florence. **Gianni, silence please!** In Florence he entered the sculptor Verrocchio's studio where he learnt to model clay, paint and draw...

An adventurous invitation

Listen Archimedes, I know you're afraid of me but I want to make a proposal. I'm sure you are the one boy in the class who is really interested in getting to know Leonardo da Vinci. This machine here isn't only a model of a tank but it's a time machine and if we really want to we can travel in time. Do you want to try? Come on, let's sit in here and when I say GO think about Leonardo and you'll see what an adventure we'll have!

Archimedes listens to Mira's strange offer. Certainly the idea of travelling in time and getting to know Leonardo is irresistible. Even though he doesn't really believe it's possible, you never know with Mira, she might do some magic. He looks around. His school friends are all looking in the teacher's direction and no one is looking at them. So he sits down beside Mira in the machine and at GO thinks about how beautiful it would be if it were really true, if ....

He turns his head and everything around him goes dark, he hears a noise like a whistle which gets louder and louder and then: BANG!

An attic in Florence

Silence. **Atchoo !!**

A sneeze, what a lot of dust! Mira and Archimedes look around them. They are in a dark room, full of strange machines, a bit like the ones in the museum but more fragile. A dead bat is hanging with his wings wide open and there is the skeleton of a giant wing underneath it. Mira is delighted. Her grandmother had often told her that travelling in time was for adults and that she certainly wouldn't have been able to do it as she needed to have a lot more experience dealing with magic... Here we are. It wasn't difficult, in actual fact it was as easy as catching a tram.

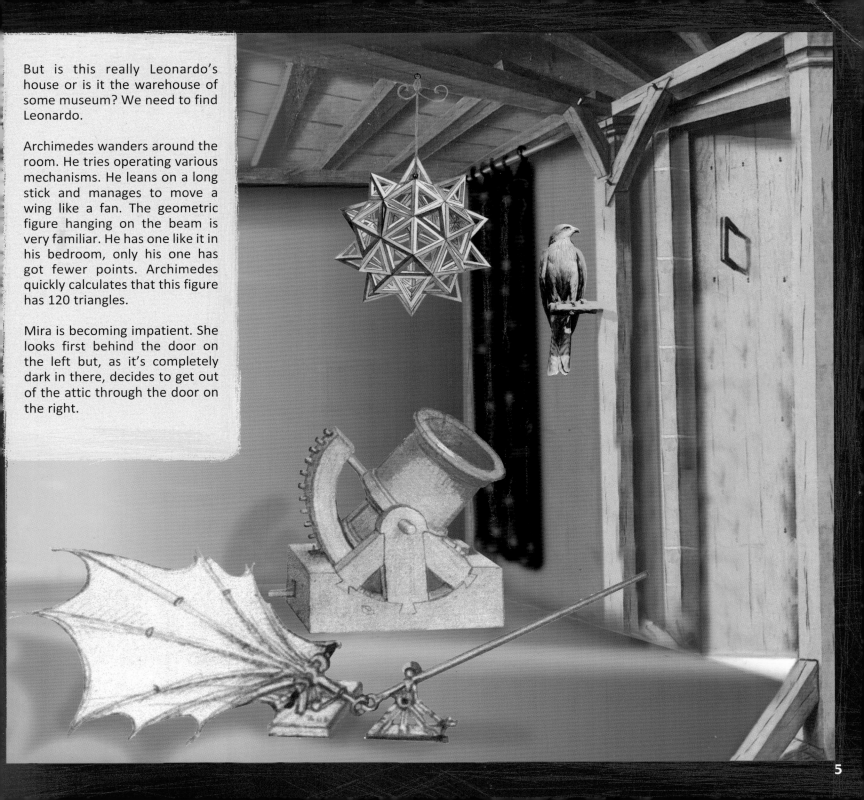

But is this really Leonardo's house or is it the warehouse of some museum? We need to find Leonardo.

Archimedes wanders around the room. He tries operating various mechanisms. He leans on a long stick and manages to move a wing like a fan. The geometric figure hanging on the beam is very familiar. He has one like it in his bedroom, only his one has got fewer points. Archimedes quickly calculates that this figure has 120 triangles.

Mira is becoming impatient. She looks first behind the door on the left but, as it's completely dark in there, decides to get out of the attic through the door on the right.

5

The painting studio

Slowly and silently they go down the wooden ladder. Mira opens the first door on the landing. It's a painter's studio. A woman sitting in the room welcomes them with a smile. Archimedes recognises the portrait on the easel. It's the Gioconda, one of the most famous paintings in the world, painted by Leonardo, and that woman is Mona Lisa. The children ask Mona Lisa where they can find Leonardo but she says nothing and just smiles mysteriously as if she hasn't understood the question. Mira closes the door again.

On opening the next door they find themselves face to face with Leonardo. He isn't as old as he appears in the portrait in the museum, but he has the same long hair and bushy beard. Leonardo is very surprised at this strange visit and doesn't understand where these two unknown children have come from. All his life he has been studying everything he sees around him and by now he knows that every phenomenon has a logical reason. But this is an extraordinary fact, is it magic?

Hello Mr. Leonardo. My name is Mira and he is called Archimedes by his schoolfriends because he likes inventing things. We have come to visit you because Archimedes wanted to get to know you a little better. You know, there are many books that talk about you but seeing you is another thing. So I tried and - as you can see - I have managed to travel in time. We come from the 21st century. What year are we in now?

Stop, wait, what are you saying, who are you, how is it possible, it isn't possible, where do you come from? You're confusing me. From the future? Do they still talk about me? What did you say, there are many books about me? This is good news, so it isn't all useless... I'll tell you what we'll do. I'll show you who I am but in exchange I'd like to know about the future from you. Oh, you have made me very curious.

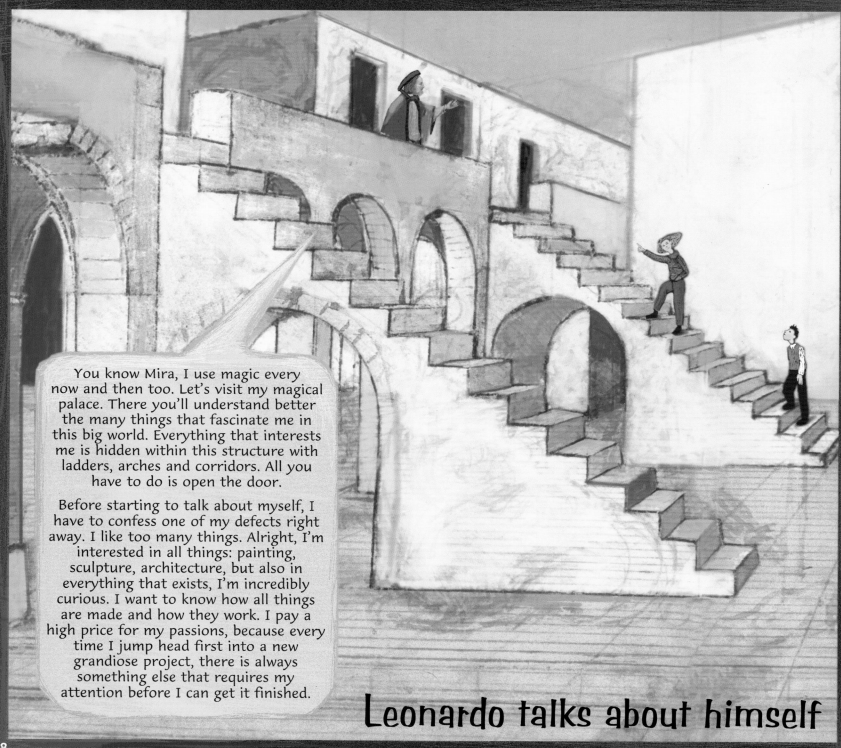

You know Mira, I use magic every now and then too. Let's visit my magical palace. There you'll understand better the many things that fascinate me in this big world. Everything that interests me is hidden within this structure with ladders, arches and corridors. All you have to do is open the door.

Before starting to talk about myself, I have to confess one of my defects right away. I like too many things. Alright, I'm interested in all things: painting, sculpture, architecture, but also in everything that exists, I'm incredibly curious. I want to know how all things are made and how they work. I pay a high price for my passions, because every time I jump head first into a new grandiose project, there is always something else that requires my attention before I can get it finished.

Leonardo talks about himself

The dream of flying

Leonardo leads the children down a long corridor: on both the right and the left there are closed doors painted in different colours. Leonardo stops in front of the third one: "Do you want to see what I am most interested in?" "Of course" answer both Archimedes and Mira. So Leonardo opens the door and suddenly they all find themselves on a hill at sunset.

One thing I've always dreamt of is being able to fly like a bird. I love the swallows, which are light creatures, that weightlessly circle in the air. When I can I go to the market and buy birds in cages. I get such satisfaction from coming here on this hill to free the prisoners. I have thoroughly studied flight and wings and I am sure that one day I will be able to make a machine that will allow man to fly. Ah, you come from the future; you can surely tell me if man will fly...

Just think how strange it is, that Leonardo has never seen an aeroplane or a helicopter.

The marvels of nature

As soon as the birds have flown past the horizon, they are back in the corridor. Archimedes points at a big violet-coloured door. Leonardo warns:
"You aren't afraid of a little breeze, are you?"
and opens the door. They are on the side of a mountain. The wind is howling and they have to hold on tightly so as not to fall down. Archimedes feels dizzy, but before he can even complain they are already back in front of the door, which slams shut.
Now Leonardo opens an emerald green trapdoor. They all lean over to look inside.

I love nature, wild mountains with steep cliffs. Such a grandiose and immense nature makes us realise how small we are. This is the landscape I like as a background for my paintings. A landscape where you can get lost in mountains that rise out from the middle of clouds and disappear on the horizon…

Look how deep it is! I'm afraid!

Don't worry Archimedes, this is only a painting; this landscape doesn't exist.

Nature on a small scale

Look inside this herbarium. The beauty of nature is that, on the one hand it is so immense and grandiose, and on the other it is so infinitely detailed in its small things. Look at a cricket, what a perfect machine it is, and how has the snail built its beautiful house? If you look closely at everything you can only be amazed by its perfection.

It's true. He would love to look at these insects under my microscope! Leonardo doesn't even know what a microscope is, because Galileo will invent it in a hundred years' time.

Archimedes, don't mix things. You are here to get to know Leonardo but you can't teach him everything about future inventions.

The field of horses

After the trapdoor has been closed, Mira and Archimedes look curiously at Leonardo. He gets up and signals them to follow him. Archimedes asks him how many doors there are and if there is one for every idea, but Leonardo is so busy choosing which one to open next that he isn't even listening. After some time he stops and opens an unimportant looking door. They are immediately in a meadow, surrounded by strange pencil-sketched horses.

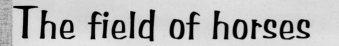

I really like horses; they are majestic animals. In order to use them in my drawings, I come on this field and draw them in every position possible. I have done hundreds of drawings of horses. I needed many of these sketches for a project I was working on, once. I had already prepared the whole model to make a fantastic bronze statue of a horse, but unfortunately the model was destroyed during the war and then the project was forgotten about. But come on, I want to talk about happier things.

Back again in the corridor, Leonardo sits down on a low wall. Archimedes notices that the index finger of his left hand is all black, and asks him why. Instead of answering, Leonardo takes the children into a room of his magical palace. The room is packed with sheets of paper, and in mid air appear drawings of cogwheels and strange contraptions.

As soon as I can I always try to find some time for myself, in solitude. It's the only way I can let my thoughts flow freely, without having to explain anything to anybody. I often feel the need to write down what I'm thinking, and that's why I always carry a notebook. Look, I write everything in here. I don't like people nosing in my writings, so I write backwards, from right to left, in a way that most people find difficult to read. It comes naturally to me to write in this way, since I'm left-handed.

Writing left-handed

Cogwheels

All my science is here in these notebooks. Just think: I could fill entire rooms with my inventions. Yes, I have designed all kinds of things: once I was at the service of the Duke of Milan, Lodovico il Moro, have you ever heard of him? I made war machines for him, and also contraptions for the court shows. Archimedes, I want to tell you one of my secrets. The wheels, the gears, yes, the transmission, you probably understand, that's the base of all machines.

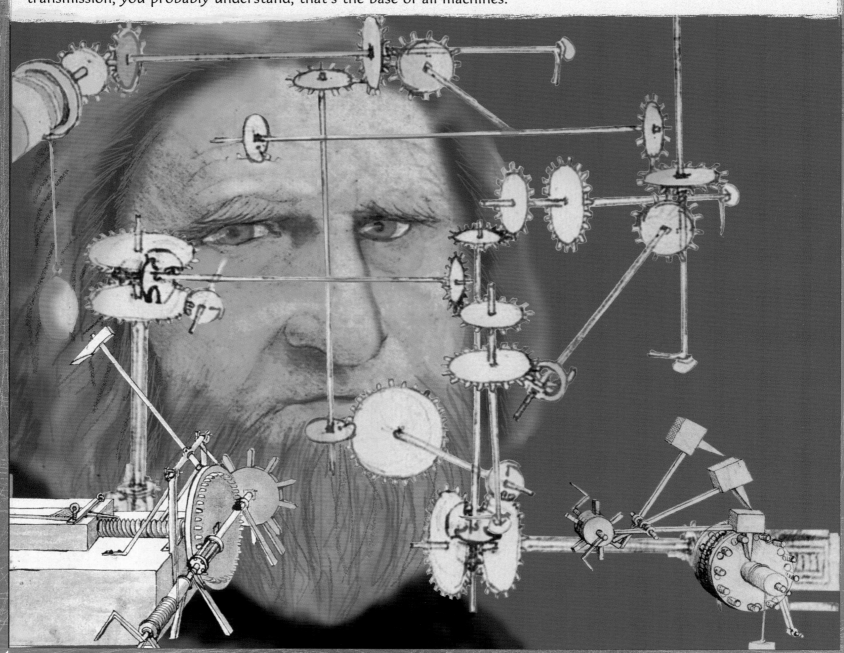

Painting, what a passion

They eventually leave the magical palace and go back to Leonardo's studio, where Mona Lisa is patiently waiting for the painter to get back to his work.

I learnt this beautiful art of painting when I was young. It is the most sublime of all arts. In this portrait of Mona Lisa I'm painting, I am trying to reach perfection. I paint all the shapes which are tinged by light and I bring them out from the darkness. That's why I need a dark background like the one behind Lisa. **Hey Lisa, don't go to sleep!** Alright, that's enough for today, Lisa. I still have to show something to my young friends. Come on, I'll show you Florence!

Here we are, this is the main square in Florence, and that is the Palazzo della Signoria. Next year in the Main Hall of the palace I'll paint a battle of the Florentines against the Milanese. I've already started to make some sketches. Just yesterday I heard that Michelangelo will make a fresco next to mine. I can't wait to see what that sculptor will get up to with the brushes! It will be a great challenge. I'd like to try and paint with wax colours, so that the tones will be warmer and denser. Yes, I'll do such a special job of it that everyone will have to agree that nobody can be compared to me, Leonardo da Vinci, painter and inventor!

Better not tell him that he won't finish this job either, if I remember rightly.

I could still talk for hours about the water and the wind, how children are born..... But then, what can you tell me? You come from such a distant time, who knows how different things will be, and how many things will have been discovered. Tell me, is there still war?
The thing that I would like most would be to come with you and have a look around.
I think that is the only way I could envision it, do you think it's possible, Mira?

Well, let's try. We can go back the way we came, the time machine is in the attic.

But Mr. Leonardo, Man has invented many new things, maybe too many...

17

Back again in the museum

Mira, are you sure that there's a logic to how this machine moves? Can you explain how it works?

I'm sorry, Mr. Leonardo, but it's a family secret. Look, this room of the museum is completely dedicated to your inventions!

We are back!

After having spent the whole day in far-away 1503 in Leonardo's house, it is night when they come back. There isn't a living soul in the museum when the three get out of this strange means of transport. Mira is a bit worried. Maybe it wasn't such a good idea to bring Leonardo back with them. A journey 500 years into the future can drive one crazy. Better to stay in the museum, where at least the inventions exhibited don't move. Archimedes is enthusiastic. Now he can show Leonardo all the fantastic things that have been invented over the last centuries, and he will be the one to illustrate how the machines work.

Leonardo is amazed

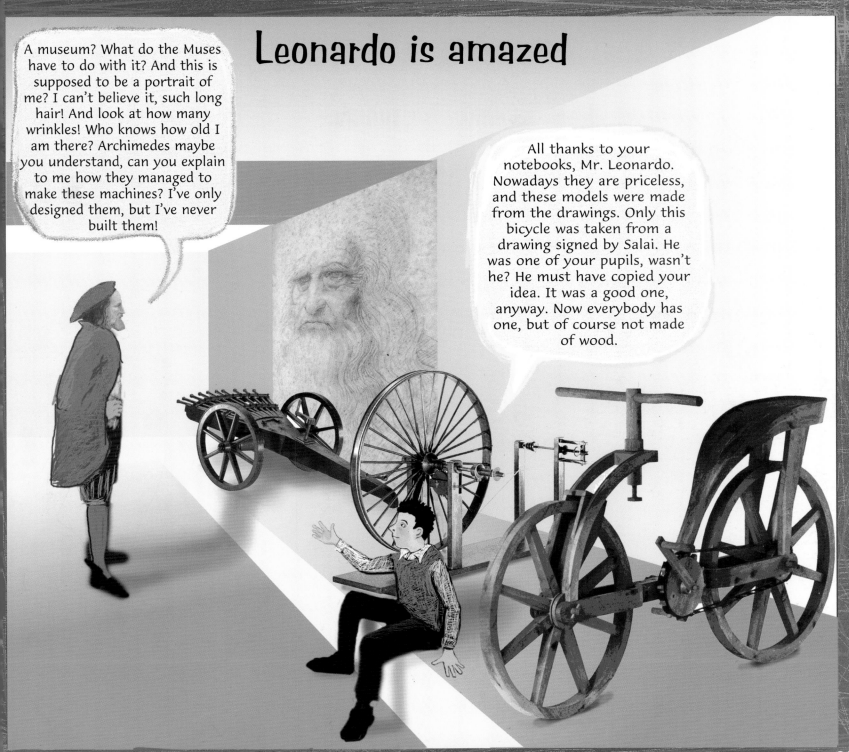

In the aeroplane hall Leonardo really starts to go out of his mind. He jumps up and down like a madman shouting Yes! Yes! Archimedes tries to keep up with him so as to explain the chronology of the inventions on flight but Leonardo doesn't even listen.

Leonardo runs around the museum and in the end he goes out through a service door. Imagine the fright! On the road he sees the lights of the moving cars, the noise of a big city which certainly isn't the Milan he knows... Mira manages to stop him on the footpath. He is so bewildered that he makes no resistance when she brings him back inside the museum to the room of the machines.